CONTENTS

Any words appearing in the text in bold, **like this**, are explained in the glossary. You can also look out for them in the Word Bank box at the bottom of each page.

THE LONGEST DAY

What led to war?

In 1933, the **Nazi** party, led by Adolf Hitler, came to power in Germany. Hitler promised to reclaim all the lands Germany had lost at the end of World War I in 1918. His attempt to do so, and to make Germany a world power again, led to a second world war. More than any other leader, Adolf Hitler was responsible for starting World War II.

Leonard Lommel and the rest of the US 2nd Ranger **battalion** fell silent as their boat approached the beach near Point du Hoc, France. Their mission was to climb the 30-metre (100-foot) cliffs and destroy three large German gun positions. Their task was vital to the success of the whole operation. If not destroyed, the German **artillery** could wipe out the American troops arriving on the beach below.

Bravery through pain

Lommel's mission did not start well. As he exited his landing craft, Lommel was shot through the right side of his body. Although he was in terrible pain, he carried on running to the bottom of the steep cliffs.

US troops leave their landing craft on D-Day, the massive **Allied** invasion of Normandy, France. It is the largest invasion by sea in history. The invasion date of 6 June 1944 is often referred to as "the longest day". ↓

Word Bank   artillery   large guns that fire shells or missiles
battalion   large military unit made up of 300 to 1000 troops

On the Front Line

UNDER FIRE IN WORLD WAR II

Brian Fitzgerald

www.raintreepublishers.co.uk

Visit our website to find out more information about **Raintree** books.

To order:
☎ Phone 44 (0) 1865 888113
▤ Send a fax to 44 (0) 1865 314091
💻 Visit the Raintree Bookshop at **www.raintreepublishers.co.uk** to browse our catalogue and order online.

Produced for Raintree by
White-Thomson Publishing Ltd
Bridgewater Business Centre
210 High Street, Lewes, BN7 2NH.

First published in Great Britain by Raintree,
Halley Court, Jordan Hill, Oxford OX2 8EJ,
part of Harcourt Education.
Raintree is a registered trademark of
Harcourt Education Ltd.

Editorial: Juliet Smith and Daniel Nunn
Design: Michelle Lisseter and Clare Nicholas
Picture Research: Amy Sparks
Project manager: Juliet Smith
Production: Duncan Gilbert

Originated by Dot Gradations Ltd
Printed and bound in China by South China Printing Company Ltd

ISBN 1 844 43691 8 (hardback)
09 08 07 06 05
10 9 8 7 6 5 4 3 2 1

ISBN 1 844 43698 5 (paperback)
10 09 08 07 06
10 9 8 7 6 5 4 3 2 1

British Library Cataloguing in Publication Data
Fitzgerald, Brian
Under Fire in World War II. – (On the Front Line)
1. World War, 1939–1945 – Juvenile literature
I. Title 940.5
A full catalogue record for this book is available from the British Library.

Acknowledgements
The publishers would like to thank the following for permission to reproduce photographs:
AKG pp. **4–5**, **6**, **9**, **12**(r), **14**, **15**, **17**, **23**, **26**(l), **31**, **34**(r), **36**(l), **36–37**, **41**(l), **41**(r); Corbis pp. **8**, **12**(l), **18–19**, **20**, **22**, **24**, **25**, **29**, **30**, **32**, **33**, **34**(l), **35**, **38**, **40**; Harcourt pp. **4**(l), **18**(l), **39**; Popperfoto pp. **10**, **11**, **27**; Topfoto pp. **title page**, **13**, **16**, **19**(r), **21**, **26**(r), **28**.
Cover photograph of US troops landing on a Normandy beach in France on 6 June 1944, reproduced with kind permission of Corbis.

Maps on pp. 7, 22 by Peter Bull.

Source notes: p. **8** Fowler's account taken from *Many Kinds of Courage: An Oral History of World War II* by Richard Lidz; p. **13** Patricia Hardy quote taken from *Put that Light Out! Memories of Childhood in Wartime London*, available at: http://www.macksites.com/light.htm; p. **14** Number of ships sunk taken from *Official History*; *War at Sea* vol. 1–3, published in *Battle of the Atlantic* by Terry Hughes and John Costello; p. **17** Quote from Henry Metalmann taken from his memoir *Through Hell with Hitler*; pp. **28–29** The account of Vassili Zaitsev's exploits is taken from his autobiography *Notes of a Sniper*; p. **32** Main text based on an edited transcript taken from an interview drawn from the oral history project at the Eisenhower Center for American Studies in New Orleans; pp. **34–35** Main text: *Band of Brothers* by Stephen Ambrose; p. **41** Quote taken from Junji Sarashina from *The Century* by Peter Jennings and Tom Brewster.

The cliffs were wet from the rain, and Lommel's rope was muddy and very slippery. As he climbed, German soldiers fired on him and threw **grenades** from above. When Lommel reached the top of the cliffs, he got a terrible shock. The big German guns were not there.

Success

Lommel and another Ranger, Jack Kuhn, went to look for the guns. They discovered five large German guns, called **howitzers,** and were surprised to find that the guns were not being guarded. Kuhn kept watch as Lommel placed grenades on each of the howitzers. Both soldiers were thrown through the air by the explosion that followed, but they were not hurt. The German guns were destroyed, but the small victory had come with a heavy price. More than half of the 225 Rangers in Lommel's unit had been killed or seriously wounded.

Find out later

In which Soviet city did Germany suffer a catastrophic defeat?

Where did these US soldiers get captured?

What were these shelters called?

grenades weapons filled with explosives that can be thrown at a target
howitzer cannon on wheels that is pulled into place by a tractor or jeep

BLITZKRIEG!

On 1 September 1939, Germany invaded Poland. The Germans used tanks and **dive-bombers** to attack their neighbour. They called this new type of warfare "blitzkrieg", or "lightning war", because the attacks were very fast. The United Kingdom and France had promised to defend Poland if Germany invaded, so both nations declared war on Germany. World War II had begun.

The "Phoney War"

Hitler shocked the **Allies** by making a deal with his enemy, Josef Stalin, the **Communist** leader of the **Soviet Union** (also called the USSR). Germany and the Soviet Union agreed to split Poland between them. After Poland fell, the Germans took a break to prepare for the more difficult invasion of countries to the west. France and the United Kingdom used this time to strengthen their own defences. This period of little fighting became known as the "Phoney War".

German soldiers rest on a **howitzer** during a pause in fighting on the Polish border.

Word Bank   Communist someone who supports the political idea that government should own all land and industry

The German advance continues

On 10 May 1940, the Germans swept into Luxembourg, Belgium, and the Netherlands. They surprised the Allies by making their main attack through the thick forests of the Ardennes region. Luxembourg fell in one day. The Netherlands surrendered in five days. Belgium held on for less than three weeks. The fast-moving German army then began to invade France. They wanted to cut the Allies' defences in half and trap the British. The Allied armies had to retreat to the French port of Dunkirk.

Winston Churchill
On 10 May 1940, Winston Churchill became Prime Minister of Britain . Three days later he told the British **Parliament**:

"I have nothing to offer but blood, toil, tears and sweat."

This map shows the borders of Europe at the start of World War II in 1939.

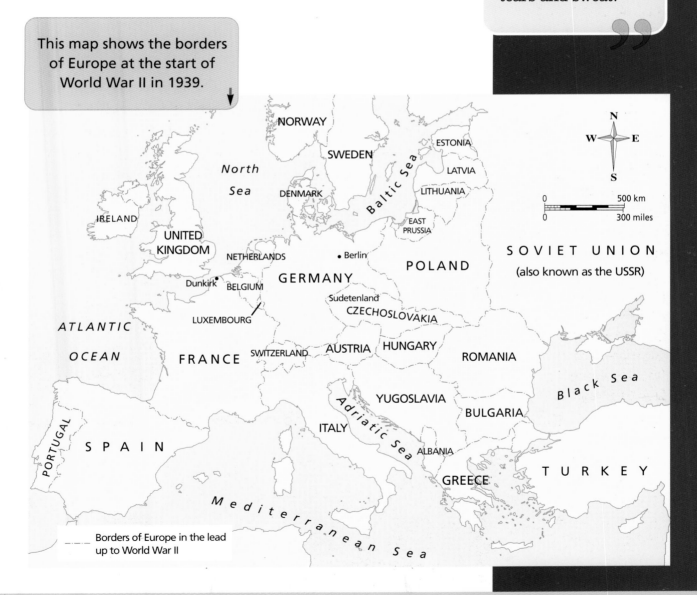

Borders of Europe in the lead up to World War II

Soviet Union country that once spread across northern Asia into Eastern Europe and included what is now Russia. Also known as the USSR

Miracle at Dunkirk

Dunkirk could have been a terrible defeat for the **Allies**, but it became a great moral victory instead. In nine days, more than 338,000 Allied troops were **evacuated**. Unfortunately, they left more than 100,000 vehicles and tons of **ammunition** and supplies behind.

Dunkirk

With much of northern France captured by the Germans, the British army either had to escape or be destroyed. On the evening of 1 June 1940, Sergeant John Fowler joined other British troops marching to the beach at Dunkirk in France. The Germans pounded the road ahead with bombs. Fowler reached the beach at about 2 a.m. as German planes flew overhead. The men lay perfectly still on the wet sand. They did not want to give their enemy anything to fire at.

The following morning Fowler joined a long queue that stretched into the water. The men passed stretchers with wounded **comrades** over their heads towards waiting rescue boats. Not all the boats were military ships. Motorboats, fishing boats, ferries, and sailboats were also used. Meanwhile, German planes fired at the British troops, who had nowhere to hide.

Hundreds of trapped British and French troops wait to be rescued from the beach at Dunkirk.

Word Bank   ammunition materials that are fired from a weapon
armistice formal agreement to stop fighting

Swimming to survive

Fowler knew his best chance for survival was to swim for it. A **corporal** from his unit could not swim, so Fowler carried him on his back and swam out to one of the rescue boats. The boat took them out to a destroyer, called the *Ivanhoe*. But Fowler was not safe for long. The *Ivanhoe* was soon hit by a bomb. He abandoned ship and swam to yet another boat. Eventually, the boat reached the English port of Dover. Fowler was finally back home.

German troops parade down the Champs-Elysées, the most famous street in Paris, having captured the French capital in June 1940.

France falls to Germans

On 22 June 1940, the French Prime Minister signed an **armistice** with the Germans. A small portion of southern France, called Vichy France, was allowed to govern itself. The **Nazis** controlled the rest of the country.

---

corporal soldier who ranks above a private but below a sergeant
evacuate bring to safety

THE UNITED KINGDOM ALONE

With the defeat of France in June 1940, the United Kingdom became the last obstacle to Germany's control of Europe. The German leader, Adolf Hitler, wanted to invade England, but he needed to weaken the British air force first. This meant that the Battle of Britain would be fought in the skies. However, the British had fewer than 700 fighters to defend their homeland against 2600 **Luftwaffe** fighter and bombers.

Air battle

On 16 August 1940, Royal Air Force (RAF) pilot James Nicholson raced to his Hurricane to intercept a group of German planes. He and two other pilots from Squadron 249 met the German aircraft over the English coast, near Southampton. As they moved in for the kill, the Hurricanes were surprised by another group of German fighters.

RAF fighter pilots race to their planes for another mission in the skies against the Luftwaffe during the Battle of Britain in 1940. ↓

Word Bank Luftwaffe the German air force

Direct hits

Both of Nicholson's **wingmen** were hit. One flew off to bring his damaged plane back home. The other jumped out of his burning plane. Nicholson's fuel tank was hit. His plane also burst into flames. Nicholson was about to parachute out when he spotted an enemy fighter.

Refusal to quit

The flames had begun to burn Nicholson, but he bravely decided to attack. The young pilot fired his machine guns, and the enemy fighter fell from the sky. Though he was badly injured, Nicholson escaped from the blazing plane. He was later awarded Britain's highest honour, the Victoria Cross, for his bravery.

Foreign fliers

British RAF pilots had help from more than 500 foreign pilots during the Battle of Britain. Airmen from Poland, Canada, New Zealand, the United States, and Jamaica were among those who joined the fight against the Luftwaffe.

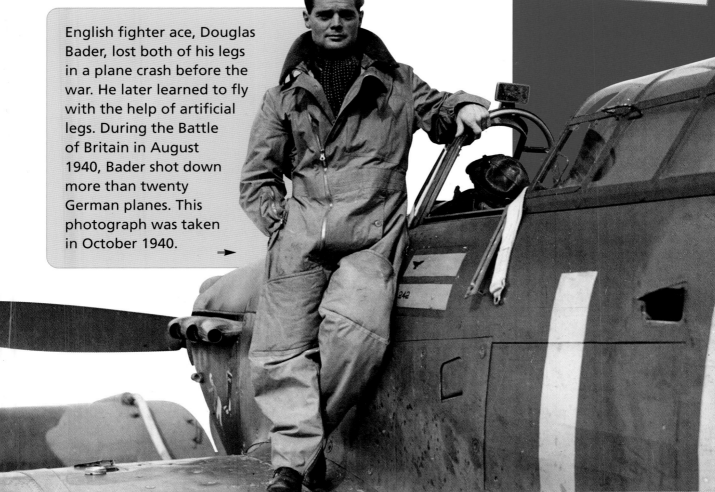

English fighter ace, Douglas Bader, lost both of his legs in a plane crash before the war. He later learned to fly with the help of artificial legs. During the Battle of Britain in August 1940, Bader shot down more than twenty German planes. This photograph was taken in October 1940. ➡

wingmen   pilots who fly behind the leader of a flying formation of planes

11

The London Blitz

On 24 August 1940, German planes dropped bombs on London, the capital of England. Winston Churchill responded by ordering RAF bombers to attack Berlin, the capital of Germany. This made Hitler very angry. Earlier German bombing raids had been aimed at military targets. Now the Germans would attempt to destroy the determination of the British people by bombing their cities.

Constant bombing

Beginning in early September 1940, more than 250 German bombers flew raids over London each night. Each raid left many **civilians** dead or injured. Whole areas of the city went up in flames. The streets were filled with bomb **craters** and debris from fallen buildings. Thousands of Londoners found safety by sleeping in underground train stations.

Barrage balloons

Giant balloons, called barrage balloons, helped protect London from attack. The steel cables that held the balloons could tear an enemy fighter apart. The high-flying balloons also forced **Luftwaffe** bombers to fly higher. This made it harder for them to hit their targets. The women pictured below had the important job of operating the barrage balloons that protected the skies over the United Kingdom.

German bombing raids during the Blitz left much of London in ruins. Luckily, St Paul's Cathedral (pictured in the background below) survived.

Word Bank   civilian   someone who is not part of the military

Invasion is defeated

Hitler hoped to bring the United Kingdom to its knees. Instead, the bombings had the opposite effect. The British suffered greatly: more than 23,000 civilians were killed between July and December 1940. However, this made the British people more determined than ever not to let the Germans win.

The RAF continued to destroy German planes. Between July and October 1940, RAF fighters shot down 1733 German aircraft. The Germans had to give up their plan of invading the United Kingdom. For the first time Germany had been defeated, but the United Kingdom also paid a heavy price. More than 900 RAF aircraft had been lost and 415 pilots had been killed.

Child of the Blitz

Patricia Hardy was nine years old during the Blitz. She remembers the terror of being bombed:

"We emerged from the shelter the next morning – it had been a terrible night. In the school playing field there was a bomb crater which you could have got a double-decker bus in, and all around were bombed houses."

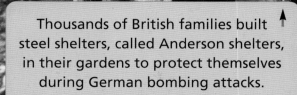

Thousands of British families built steel shelters, called Anderson shelters, in their gardens to protect themselves during German bombing attacks.

crater   huge hole left when a bomb hits the ground and explodes

GERMANY ON THE ATTACK

Ships sunk

Huge numbers of **Allied** ships were sunk by German U-boats during the war:

Year		Number
1939	–	114
1940	–	471
1941	–	432
1942	–	1160
1943	–	377
1944	–	56
1945	–	55

In October 1939, the Germans planned a daring **U-boat** attack. Their target was the British naval base at Scapa Flow in the Orkney Islands, Scotland. Sinking a warship anchored at the base would be a huge victory for the Germans. Getting past the British defences would require great bravery and skill.

U-47 takes to the sea

On 8 October, the captain of submarine U-47, Günther Prien, gave the order to head for Scapa Flow. After more than five days of manoeuvring past **blockades**, sunken ships and terrible tides, the submarine finally reached the naval base. The U-boat stayed under water during the day. At night, it would be able to surface and sail toward its targets.

A torpedo from a U-boat strikes the British steamer, *Beluchistan*, off the coast of West Africa in March 1942.

Word Bank   battleship   large and heavily armoured warship

Unfortunately for Prien, the Northern Lights filled the sky, meaning the port was well-lit even at night. "It is disgustingly light," Prien wrote in his ship's diary. "The whole bay is lit up." This made it difficult for the U-47 to travel into the harbour safely.

Direct hit

Nevertheless, U-47 managed to move quietly past a coastguard patrol. Ahead were two **battleships**. Prien's crew quickly got the **torpedoes** ready and fired. "There is a loud explosion, roar and rumbling," Prien recorded. "Then come columns of water, followed by columns of fire and splinters flying through the air." The great British battleship, *Royal Oak*, had been sunk. The U-47 escaped from the harbour without being noticed.

Happy time

During the Battle of Britain, the Royal Navy helped to protect the United Kingdom from invasion. This left supply ships open to attack. From July to October 1940, German submarines sank more than a million tons of shipping. German sailors called this their "happy time". The year 1942 became known as their "second happy time" because they sunk even more ships than in 1940.

A German U-boat surfaces in the English Channel in 1940, after a successful hunt for Allied shipping in the Atlantic.

U-boat   type of German submarine
torpedo   missile that is fired underwater

Siege of Leningrad

In September 1941, the Germans surrounded Leningrad (now called St Petersburg) in Russia and cut off **supply routes** to the city. More than 600,000 people died from starvation and German bombings. The Germans were finally pushed back in January 1944.

Invasion of Russia

Once Germany's invasion of the United Kingdom had been defeated, Hitler looked instead to his other great target – the **Soviet Union**. Despite his agreement with Stalin, Hitler hated **Communism**. He also wanted the Soviet Union's **natural resources** for Germany. In June 1941, more than three million German troops and 3000 tanks swept into the Soviet Union. The war front spanned 2000 miles.

The Soviet Union's Red Army was caught by surprise. Hundreds of thousands of Soviet troops were surrounded and forced to surrender. **Luftwaffe** pilots destroyed hundreds of Soviet aircraft on the ground. By the end of September 1941, Stalin had lost more than two million men.

Germans tanks charge across the Soviet countryside in the summer of 1941.

Word Bank   natural resources   usefulmaterials in nature that are helpful to humans, such as coal, oil, and minerals

Brave resistance

Despite this early disaster, the Soviet people refused to give up. As they left their farms and cities, the Soviets burned their own crops and destroyed their own homes. They did not want to leave behind anything that the Germans could use. The Soviet army had lost countless men, but was still huge. The Soviets could afford to lose five of their own men to kill one German.

Nature helps

The weather also worked against the Germans because they were not prepared for the harsh Soviet winter. They did not have winter clothes and their weapons froze and would not work. Also, the Germans' vehicles could not move in the snow and mud. Their rapid advance came to a halt.

> **Severe cold**
> Henry Metalmann was a German tank driver. Here he remembers the Russian winter of 1941:
> "It was so cold you couldn't even touch metal with your bare skin because the skin would stick to the metal. When it's that cold you reach a point where you don't care any more whether you live or die."

German troops faced heavy snow and freezing temperatures during the Soviet winter of 1941–1942.

The United Kingdom was running out of weapons and supplies. Winston Churchill asked the United States to support the war effort, but many Americans did not want to get involved in an expensive war overseas.

Support for an ally

US President Franklin Roosevelt knew the United Kingdom needed help. If Germany defeated the United Kingdom, the United States would be the last great **democracy** left in the world. Early in the war, the United States had sold weapons and supplies to the United Kingdom. But the British no longer had enough money to pay for these materials. So, in March 1941, Roosevelt agreed to lend the United Kingdom all the war material it needed to continue the fight.

Lend-Lease Act

The US Lend-Lease programme provided aircraft, ships and **ammunition** to the United Kingdom and later the Soviet Union. By the end of the war, the United States had given about $50 billion in war materials to its **Allies**.

We Can Do It!

WAR PRODUCTION CO-ORDINATING COMMITTEE

Poster campaigns like "Rosie the Riveter" (above) encouraged American women to join the war effort.

Word Bank alliance agreement to work together
democracy system in which people can elect their leaders

Both countries also pledged to help the **Soviet Union**. Even though the United Kingdom and the United States were enemies of **Communism**, they considered the **Nazis** to be an even greater enemy.

Trouble in the Far East

Roosevelt was also worried about Japan. This island nation did not have the land or **resources** to support its people. Its military government chose to take what it needed by force. Japan had already invaded its neighbour, China, in 1937. In 1940, Japan moved troops into Northern Indochina (now called Vietnam) to block supply shipments to China. This caused the United States to cut off trade with Japan. The Japanese Prime Minister, Hideki Tojo, decided to act against the United States. Japan began to prepare a surprise attack.

Axis powers

On 27 September 1940, leaders from Japan, Italy and Germany officially formed an **alliance** by signing the Tripartite Pact. The three nations agreed to co-operate in their planned invasions of other countries. Together, these three nations became known as the "Axis powers".

US factories produced a huge amount of war materials. This factory in Stanford, Connecticut, made more than 6000 fighter planes during World War II.

Italy's Benito Mussolini (left) and Germany's Adolf Hitler (right) wanted to conquer all of Europe.

resources useful materials, such as oil or metals

"A date which will live in infamy"

On 7 December 1941, Dorie Miller rose at 6 a.m. to serve breakfast to the crew of the USS *West Virginia*. The young cook was also busy collecting laundry when an explosion rocked the ship. The *West Virginia* and the rest of the American fleet at Pearl Harbor, Hawaii, were under attack. Miller ran to his **battle station**. He found that it had been damaged by a Japanese **torpedo** so he went up to the ship's deck to see if he could help. The smoke was so thick that it was hard for him to see. Fire burned everywhere. Even the water in the harbour was in flames!

Surprise attack!

The surprise Japanese attack on Pearl Harbor lasted two hours and included 353 Japanese planes. The damage was terrible. The attack killed 2403 Americans and wounded 1178. Japanese planes managed to sink or badly damage eighteen US ships. Nearly 170 US planes were also destroyed.

This rare photo shows Japanese **dive-bombers** preparing to take off for the attack on Pearl Harbor.

Word Bank   anti-aircraft guns   weapons on the ground or on board ships that are used to fire at enemy planes

Right man for the job

An officer asked for Miller's help. The ship's captain had been seriously injured and needed to be moved. Miller was the ship's boxing champion and one of its strongest men. He carried the captain to safety. Sadly, the captain died soon afterwards. A sailor asked Miller to help load **ammunition** into one of the ship's **anti-aircraft guns**. Miller decided he would man the gun instead, despite the fact he did not have any training. Still he fired away at the Japanese planes that zoomed by the ship. The *West Virginia* was in flames and sinking fast. Miller and the rest of the crew were forced to abandon ship. Miller was eventually killed later in the war when another ship he was on, the USS *Liscombe Bay*, was torpedoed on 25 November 1944.

More attacks

The Japanese also launched attacks on other islands in the Pacific on 7 December 1941, including Guam, Hong Kong, and the Philippines. In a speech the following day, US President Roosevelt called 7 December "a date which will live in **infamy**".

Another ship, the USS *Arizona*, also suffered a fatal bomb strike on 7 December 1941. The great **battleship** sank to the bottom of Pearl Harbor in less than nine minutes. More than 1100 of its crewmen died that day.

battle station   a place for carrying out duties during an attack
infamy   something that is famous for being bad

WAR IN THE PACIFIC

Doolittle Raid

The photo below shows an American B-25 bomber taking off from the USS *Hornet* to take part in the Doolittle Raid. This took place on 18 April 1942, when a US pilot called Jimmy Doolittle led a daring bombing raid on Japan. It was revenge for Pearl Harbor. The raid did not do much physical damage, but it boosted US **morale**. It also showed that Japan was vulnerable to attack.

The day after the Pearl Harbor attack, the United States and the United Kingdom declared war on Japan. Germany and Italy then declared war on the United States. The United States had been lucky because none of its four **aircraft carriers** had been docked at Pearl Harbor on 7 December. Even so, the United States was not strong enough to stop the Japanese advance through Southeast Asia.

Japanese advance

The British were not prepared either. On 10 December 1941, Japanese planes sank the British warships *Prince of Wales* and *Repulse* near the Malayan coast. On Christmas Day, British troops in Hong Kong surrendered. Less than two months after that, Japanese troops took over Singapore, Britain's main Far East naval base. Japanese aircraft even managed to drop bombs on the Australian mainland, hitting Darwin on 19 February 1942.

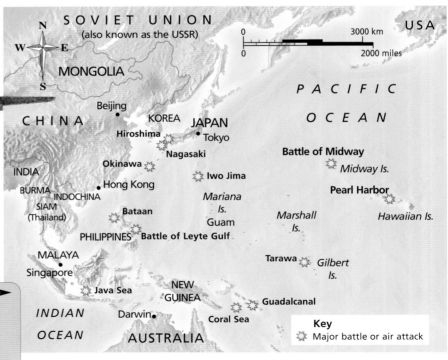

After the Pearl Harbor attack, Japan quickly captured other areas in the Pacific.

Word Bank aircraft carrier huge ship with a flat deck that acts as a runway for naval planes to take off and land

The United States is defeated

Next, the Japanese set their sights on the Philippines, which was an American colony. US and Filipino troops fought bravely, but were outnumbered. American General Douglas MacArthur was forced to leave, but promised to return (see page 38). The remaining US and Filipino troops were pushed back to the Bataan Peninsula. On 9 April 1942, 12,000 US and 64,000 Filipino troops surrendered.

Death march

The Japanese believed surrender was dishonourable. They treated prisoners of war (**POWs**) with little respect. The Americans captured at Bataan were forced to march about 104 kilometres (65 miles) to prison camps. Around 5200 US soldiers died along the way from starvation and fatigue. The Bataan Death March inspired other American troops in the region to fight even harder.

Wrongly accused

After the Pearl Harbor attack, many Americans wrongly suspected Japanese-Americans of planning attacks in the United States. They were forced to sell their homes and leave their jobs, and were then sent to **work camps**. The US **Supreme Court** ordered the camps to be closed in December 1944.

These are some of the thousands of US troops who were forced to take part in the Bataan Death March in 1942.

morale   level of confidence and determination to succeed
work camps   places where people were forced to live and work for little or no money

Guadalcanal

In July 1942, the Japanese began building an airfield on the island of Guadalcanal, in the South Pacific. **Allied** command thought that their next target was Australia. US marines landed on the tiny island in August and quickly captured the airfield. On 26 October, Sergeant Mitchell Paige and his **battalion** were sent to defend their position against 2500 Japanese troops. Working in total darkness, Paige set up four machine guns to cover the rifle companies on his left and right. Then he placed a **trip-wire** in front of the position, with **C-ration** cans attached. So now he would hear enemy troops approaching.

The Japanese attack

During the night, Paige heard a rattling from the trip-wire. He ordered his men to start firing their guns but the larger force of Japanese troops were soon upon Paige and his men.

These two American marines are firing a captured Japanese machine gun at Japanese planes during the battle for Guadalcanal in 1942. ↓

bayonet long knife that is attached to the end of a gun
C-ration soldier's meal kit

24

Throughout the early morning hours, Japanese soldiers swarmed up the hill. They fought with guns, **bayonets**, and even swords.

A brave stand

By dawn, Paige was the only member of his **platoon** left standing. He ran around firing guns from different positions. He needed the Japanese to think there were lots of men still fighting. He pulled a machine gun from its stand and ran, carrying the heavy weapon in his arms. Enemy soldiers fell all around him. Before long, the Japanese were in full retreat. They never recaptured the airfield, thanks largely to Paige's heroism.

Code busters

As early as September 1940, US forces gained an advantage over their enemy by cracking the Japanese code. Now they could "listen in" on the enemy's plans. This helped US pilots find and shoot down a plane – on 18 April 1943 – carrying Admiral Yamamoto, who had planned the Pearl Harbor attack.

Japanese soldiers man a heavy machine gun against the US forces on Guadalcanal.

trip-wire wire that is stretched close to the ground and acts as an alarm if someone touches it

THE ALLIES TURN THE TIDE

North Africa had been an important battleground since early in the war. Italy had invaded Egypt in 1940 in an attempt to take control of the Suez Canal. This would have blocked **Allied supply routes** to the Far East. British forces fought back and forced the Italians to retreat into Libya. German troops, led by Erwin Rommel, then joined the fight and pushed the British back into Egypt.

The Desert Fox

Erwin Rommel (below left) was one of the **Nazis'** most brilliant military leaders. He was known as "the Desert Fox" because he was cunning and it was difficult to guess what his next action would be.

Battle of El Alamein

The two sides came together at the Battle of El Alamein in 1942. British General Bernard Montgomery led the Allied forces. After twelve days of fierce fighting, the British and Australian troops pushed Rommel's army out of Egypt for good. It was one of the Allies' greatest victories of the war. After the victory at El Alamein, Montgomery's troops pursued Rommel west through the desert.

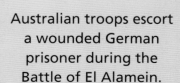

Australian troops escort a wounded German prisoner during the Battle of El Alamein.

Word Bank   casualties   people who are injured or killed in a war

Operation Torch

Less than a week after the victory at El Alamein, the Allies launched Operation Torch. US troops landed in North Africa. Their goal was to join Montgomery's forces and crush Rommel's army. But the American troops did not do well in their first battle against the Germans. Rommel's army broke through the American lines at Kasserine Pass, in Tunisia. The Americans suffered more than 3000 **casualties** and lost hundreds of trucks and tanks.

However, the US defences got tougher and the Germans were soon pushed back. By the middle of May 1943, Allied forces had taken more than 200,000 prisoners and all of North Africa was back in Allied hands.

The Allies had far more tanks than the Germans did at El Alamein. This helped them gain an advantage during the historic battle.

Battle of Stalingrad

At the same time as the **Allies** were capturing North Africa, the Russians were fighting a long, brave battle for Stalingrad, one of their key cities. Vassili Zaitsev, a Soviet **sniper**, needed patience to carry out his mission: killing as many **Nazi** officers as possible. He often let ordinary German soldiers escape so that he would not give away his position to the enemy.

Hours of waiting

Zaitsev and his partner, Nikolai Kulikov, sat in a **foxhole** for hours without shooting. Cramped, thirsty and surrounded by dead bodies, they waited and watched. Several German soldiers came and went, but the Soviets did not fire their weapons. It was only after a German machine gunner opened fire on their position that they returned fire and killed him.

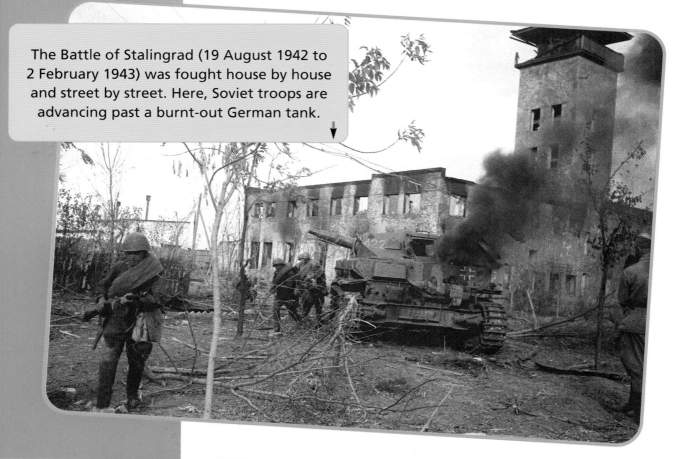

The Battle of Stalingrad (19 August 1942 to 2 February 1943) was fought house by house and street by street. Here, Soviet troops are advancing past a burnt-out German tank.

Word Bank   foxhole   shallow pit used for taking cover from enemy fire

Patience pays off

The next day, Zaitsev and Kulikov returned to an area close to their original position. By lunchtime their patience was rewarded. Two colonels, a German sniper and a major came out of hiding. Within seconds all four Nazis lay dead.

The Germans responded by firing at the snipers with **artillery**. But in doing this, they also damaged the wood panels that hid their artillery. The German soldiers were exposed and, one by one, they were picked off by the Soviets. The successful attack meant the German artillery could no longer operate during the day. Zaitsev and his team had helped turn the tide in the Battle of Stalingrad.

German surrender

The battle for Stalingrad was the bloodiest battle in history. The **Soviet Union** suffered more than a million casualties. The German 6th Army of 300,000 men was reduced to 91,000 when they surrendered. Many were sent to Soviet **work camps**. Only 6000 made it back to Germany.

In February 1943, German **POWs** walk away from the ruins of Stalingrad after their crushing defeat by Soviet forces.

sniper   hidden soldier who shoots enemy soldiers from long distances with a special gun

Anzio attack

US Sergeant Raymond Blessinger remembers his days on the beach at Anzio:

"German **artillery** pounded us day and night. We didn't want to leave our **foxholes**, but they kept filling up with rainwater. We slept on the wet sand, with only soaking wet blankets to keep us warm."

Invasion of Sicily

Following the victory in North Africa, the **Allies** decided their next target would be Sicily. This Italian island lay just across the Mediterranean Sea. The **campaign** was launched on 10 July 1943. An Allied invasion force of 180,000 troops stormed into Sicily. US General Patton's 7th Army approached from the west, while British Field Marshal Montgomery's 8th Army came from the east. The island's rocky terrain made things difficult, and the German resistance was tough. But by the middle of August, the Allies had taken Sicily and reached the Italian mainland.

US Army Rangers scramble up a hill during a battle in Italy in 1943.

Word Bank campaign series of military missions
controversial open to dispute or debate

Mussolini gets the boot

The defeat in Sicily convinced many Italians that the war was no longer worth fighting. On 25 July 1943, the Italian **dictator** Mussolini was overthrown. The Italian king then appointed a new Prime Minister, who made a peace agreement with the Allies. Within a few weeks, Italy joined the Allies and declared war on Germany.

Hitler refused to give up Italy without a fight. He rushed troops into the country to set up defences. Terrible battles followed. American troops were pinned down for four months and suffered more than 59,000 **casualties** before taking Anzio, on the west coast of Italy. The Allies needed three major assaults to take Cassino. By 5 June 1944, Allied troops had freed the Italian capital of Rome. The very next day, the Allies launched the D-Day invasion of France.

Monte Cassino

In February 1944, the Allies made a **controversial** decision to bomb the historic **monastery** at Monte Cassino, near Rome. The Allies, who knew the Germans were hiding there, destroyed everything but the cell and tomb of St Benedict.

British troops receive a warm welcome as they march through northern Italy in April 1945.

dictator person who has complete power over a country and is often cruel to those he or she rules

PATH TO VICTORY

Fake invasion

The Allies tricked the Germans into thinking they would invade Pas de Calais in the north-east of France, not Normandy in the west. They sent false radio messages about their plans. They even made fake tanks and ships that looked real to German patrol planes. Hitler moved thousands of troops to protect the area, leaving fewer troops to defend against the huge Allied invasion of Normandy.

The **Allied** invasion of France, called D-Day, was the largest and most important battle of the war. US Sergeant Thomas Valence was a part of the first wave of troops to hit Omaha Beach in Normandy, France, on D-Day. Years later he remembered: "We proceeded toward the beach, and many of the fellows got sick. The water was quite rough. When we got to the beach, or close to it, the obstacles erected by the Germans to prevent the landing were fully in view, which meant the tide was low. There was a rather wide expanse of beach, and the Germans were not to be seen at all, but they were firing at us, rapidly."

US troops arrive at a Normandy beach on D-Day on 6 June 1944.

Word Bank   paratroopers soldiers who drop into battle using parachutes

Shot in the hand

"I floundered in the water and had my hand up in the air, trying to get my balance, when I was first shot. I was shot through the left hand, which broke a knuckle, and then through the palm of the hand."

Bloody beach

"I made my way forward as best I could. I was hit again, once in the left thigh, which broke my hipbone, and a couple of times in my pack, and then my chinstrap on my helmet was severed by a bullet. I worked my way up on to the beach, and staggered up against a wall, and collapsed there. The bodies of the other guys washed ashore, and I was one live body amongst many of my friends who were dead."

Paratroopers

The Normandy invasion force was supported by 13,000 **paratroopers**. They jumped behind enemy lines the night before D-Day. Paratroopers carried more than 32 kilograms (70 pounds) of equipment, including a rifle, a compass, medical kit, Hershey chocolate bars, and chewing gum.

US paratroopers drop into France as part of the invasion of Normandy.

Battle of the Bulge

After D-Day, the **Allies** continued to push west through France. Hitler was losing ground fast. He decided to launch one last great offensive in the Ardennes region in December 1944. It became known as the Battle of the Bulge. On 29 December, US **Paratrooper** Darrell Powers and the rest of the men in his company were in the woods outside Bastogne in France. The Germans had them surrounded. For more than a week, Powers had endured freezing weather, very little food and **ammunition** and an almost constant barrage of **artillery** fire from the Germans.

Keen eyesight

Suddenly, Powers spotted a tree that he was sure had not been there the day before. He reported this to his sergeant, Carwood Lipton. Lipton looked through his **binoculars**.

US troops fought in deep snow and bitter cold during the Battle of the Bulge.

Word Bank   binoculars   hand-held instrument that allows you to see distant objects
camouflage   material that is used to hide military equipment

He noticed movement in the area. The Germans were placing artillery among the trees. The odd tree that Powers had spotted had been added as **camouflage**. Lipton called for an artillery attack on the position. The Germans quickly left the spot.

Breaking through

This was not the only time that Powers' keen eyesight helped save the lives of his **comrades**. After an attack that left a soldier in the next **foxhole paralysed**, Powers spotted a German **sniper** in a tree and shot him dead. When the paratroopers finally broke through the German line, it was Powers who found and killed the snipers who had his squad pinned down.

The German attack caught the Allies by surprise. This German tank passes a queue of American **POWs** during the first days of the Battle of the Bulge. More than 21,000 Allied troops were captured during the battle.

Germany's last offensive

The Battle of the Bulge was a major defeat for the Germans. It was also the largest battle ever fought by the US Army. Of the 600,000 US troops that took part in the fighting, 20,000 were killed and 40,000 were wounded.

paralysed   physically unable to move

Allies advance

After their victory at the Battle of the Bulge, the **Allies** pressed on. The only thing that separated the Allies from the centre of Germany was the River Rhine. Hitler ordered all bridges across the Rhine to be destroyed.

Bridge to victory

Incredibly, US troops found a bridge in the town of Remagen that was still standing. One by one, US soldiers darted across the bridge. German troops on the other side tried to blow it up, but a wire connected to their explosives had been cut. Hitler was furious when he heard the news. More than five **divisions** of US troops crossed the bridge before German troops finally blew it up.

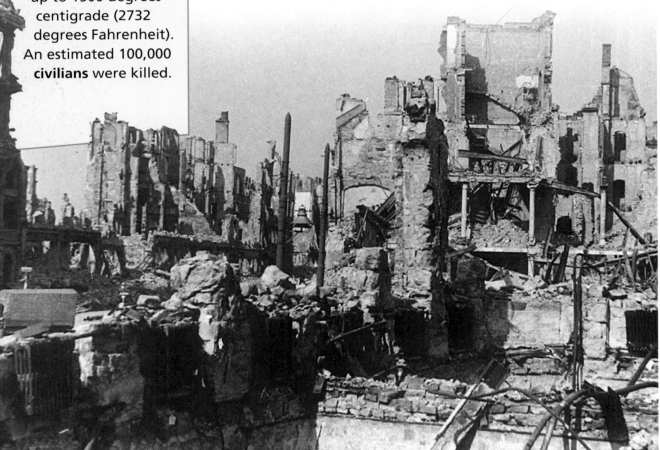

Word Bank   bunker   a shelter from bombs that is usually underground
divisions   large military units consisting of about 10,000 men

Allies meet in Germany

On 12 April 1945, US President Roosevelt died of a brain haemorrhage. But the German celebration of his death did not last long. The Soviet army had also been advancing fast. They took control of lands captured by the German army and moved into Germany itself. On 25 April 1945, the Russian and American armies met up for the first time in Torgau, Germany. The remaining German forces were now split in two.

Hitler kills himself

On 29 April 1945, Hitler married his girlfriend Eva Braun in an underground **bunker**. A day later they both committed **suicide**. One week later, German leaders surrendered to the Allies. People around the world celebrated VE (Victory in Europe) Day.

Power struggle

After D-Day, some **Nazis** realized Hitler was mad and had to be stopped. In July 1944, some German officers tried to kill Hitler with a bomb hidden inside a briefcase. But their plan failed. The men behind the plot were found and executed.

Soviet soldiers hoist their nation's flag atop the German **Parliament** building (the Reichstag) in Berlin.

suicide   act of killing oneself

THE FALL OF JAPAN

Turkey shoot

During the Battle for the Marianas Islands in June 1944, American pilots shot down nearly 400 Japanese planes in a single day. This huge US success became known as the "Marianas Turkey Shoot".

The **Allies** had won the war in Europe and were moving closer to victory in the Pacific. After capturing Guadalcanal they started a **campaign** of island-hopping. They planned to move north by capturing certain key islands. Each step took them a bit nearer to Japan. This plan allowed the Allies to save time and countless lives by bypassing some of the more heavily defended, but strategically less important, islands.

Return to the Philippines

The United States fought hard battles at New Guinea, Tarawa, and the Marshall Islands. Their next target was the Philippines. General MacArthur was keeping his earlier promise to return (see page 23). This time he brought more than 150,000 troops and 700 ships with him. Most of the battle was fought at sea, not on land.

General Douglas MacArthur wades ashore at Leyte Island, Philippines, on 20 October 1944. He had been forced to retreat from the islands in 1942 and had kept his promise, made at that time, to return.

The Battle of Leyte Gulf was the biggest naval battle ever. American warships and planes destroyed most of the Japanese fleet.

Final land battles

The last two great Pacific land battles, Iwo Jima and Okinawa (see map on page 22), were possibly the two bloodiest of the war. The United States needed both islands to launch air attacks on the Japanese mainland. The United States had planned to take Iwo Jima in less than a week. In actual fact, the fighting took almost five weeks and nearly 7000 American soldiers were killed. Similarly, on Okinawa, more than 110,000 Japanese and more than 12,000 American soldiers were killed in the three-month battle for the island.

Kamikazes

The Battle of Leyte Gulf saw the first use of kamikaze aircraft. Japanese pilots flew planes loaded with explosives directly into Allied warships. They sunk 34 ships and damaged 288 others. Nearly 4000 kamikaze pilots gave up their lives.

This famous photo shows US Marines raising the American flag on Iwo Jima.

The United States
developed the atomic
bomb because they
knew the Germans
were also trying to
create one. The project
was so secret that
President Roosevelt's
replacement, Harry
Truman, did not
even know about
it until after he
became President.

The A-bomb

As American troops continued to move from one Pacific island to the next, US bombers attacked cities within Japan. On 9–10 March 1945, US B-29 bombers dropped more than 1700 tons of bombs on Tokyo, the capital of Japan. More than 100,000 people were killed and huge areas of the city were completely destroyed.

Fighting to death

The United States hoped these terrible and destructive attacks would convince the Japanese to give up. But US military leaders realized that most Japanese people would rather fight to the death than surrender. The United States planned an invasion of Japan, but it would cost hundreds of thousands of lives. So military leaders came up with another plan.

US guns on the USS *Hornet* fire at attacking Japanese fighters as the **aircraft carrier's** bombers carry out raids on Tokyo.

The bombs are dropped

On 6 August 1945, Colonel Paul Tibbets set off on the war's most important mission. His B-29, named *Enola Gay*, carried the first atomic bomb. Shortly after 8 a.m., the *Enola Gay* dropped the bomb over the city of Hiroshima, in Japan. In a flash, most of the city was completely wiped out.

The United States dropped a second bomb on Nagasaki, Japan, three days later. The effect was just as terrible as the bomb on Hiroshima. The Japanese could not risk being hit by any more of these attacks. On 2 September 1945, the Japanese signed a formal surrender. The war was finally over.

" Ball of fire

Junji Sarashina survived the bombing of Hiroshima. Here she remembers that terrible day:

"I saw this big ball of orange fire. The whole building – and the earth itself, it seemed – moved once to the left and once to the right, and then everything started to fall on top of me."

"

These Japanese girls are wearing masks to block the smell of the dead bodies after the atomic bomb in Hiroshima.

TIMELINE

1933
30 January   Adolf Hitler becomes chancellor of Germany.

1939
1 September   Germany invades Poland.
3 September   The United Kingdom, France, New Zealand, Australia, and India declare war on Germany.
10 September   Canada joins the **Allies** and declares war on Germany.

1940
9 April   Germany invades Denmark and Norway.
10 May   Germany invades Luxembourg, Belgium, and the Netherlands.
26 May   Start of **evacuation** of British, French and Belgian troops from the beaches of Dunkirk.
10 June   Italy declares war on France and the United Kingdom.
22 June   France surrenders to Germany.
10 July   The Battle of Britain begins.
7 September   The London Blitz begins, as the **Luftwaffe** drops bombs on London and other British cities.
27 September   Japan, Germany and Italy sign the Tripartite Pact.

1941
22 June   Germany invades the **Soviet Union**.
7 December   Japanese launch a surprise attack on the US naval base at Pearl Harbor.
8 December   The United States and the United Kingdom declare war on Japan.
11 December   Germany and Italy declare war on the United States.

1942
18 April   Jimmy Doolittle leads a daring bombing raid on Japan.
4–6 June   Japanese defeated in the Battle of Midway.
7 August   The first wave of US Marines arrive on Guadalcanal and take over the Japanese airfield.
23 October   General Bernard Montgomery leads Allied troops into Battle of El Alamein.

4 November	Rommel and his troops retreat from El Alamein.
8 November	Allied invasion of North Africa, named Operation Torch, is launched.

1943

2 February	Germans surrender to the Soviet Army at Stalingrad.
10 July	Allies land on Sicily, Italy.
25 July	Benito Mussolini forced out as leader of Italy.
3 September	Italy surrenders to the Allies.

1944

22 January	US and British troops land at Anzio.
4 June	Rome falls to the Allies.
6 June	Allies launch massive invasion of Normandy (D-Day).
13 June	Germans fire V-1 flying bombs into England for the first time.
25 August	US and Free French troops enter Paris.
8 September	First V-2 flying bombs are fired against the British.
23–26 October	US victory at the Battle of Leyte Gulf marks the first use of Japanese kamikaze aircraft.
16 December	The Battle of the Bulge begins.

1945

19 February	American troops invade Iwo Jima.
1 April	American soldiers land at Okinawa.
12 April	US President Franklin Roosevelt dies. Vice President Harry Truman takes his place.
22 April	Soviet troops surround Berlin.
28 April	Benito Mussolini is murdered in Italy.
30 April	Adolf Hitler commits **suicide** in his **bunker** in Berlin.
8 May	People around the world celebrate VE Day.
6 August	The United States drops atomic bomb on Hiroshima, Japan.
9 August	Second atomic bomb dropped on Nagasaki, Japan.
15 August	VJ Day; Japanese Emperor Hirohito announces Japan's surrender to his people.
2 September	Japanese formally surrender aboard the USS *Missouri*.

FIND OUT MORE

Books

Here are just a few of the many other books about World War II:

The Battle of Britain, by Alex Woolf
Germany and Japan Attack, by Sean Sheehan
Great Battles of World War II, by Ole Steen Hansen
Leaders of World War II, by Stewart Ross
The War in the Pacific, by Peter Chrisp
(Hodder Wayland, 2000–2003)
An excellent and informative series that goes into depth on key issues/campaigns of the war.

The Good Fight: How World War II Was Won, Stephen E. Ambrose (Atheneum, 2001)
This is the one and only book for young people by the United States's great World War II expert.

The Second World War, by Christine Hatt (Evans, 2000)
Excellent use of original documents brings World War II to life.

The Second World War, by Stewart Ross (Evans, 2003)
An in-depth look at the causes and effects of World War II.

DVD/VHS

Films about World War II are often aimed at an adult audience. Ask a parent or teacher before watching these.

The World at War 30th Anniversary Edition (DVD release 2004)
Thirty years after its release, this remains the ultimate visual history of World War II.

Tora! Tora! Tora! (1970)
An epic story about the Pearl Harbor attack told from both the American and Japanese point of view.

The Great Escape (1963)
The incredible story of British and American POWs who plan a daring escape from a Nazi prison camp.

Search tips

There are billions of pages on the Internet so it can be difficult to find exactly what you are looking for. These search skills will help you find useful websites more quickly:

- Use simple keywords instead of whole sentences.

- Use two to six keywords in a search, putting the most important words first.

- Be precise – only use names of people, places or things.

- If you want to find words that go together, put quote marks around them.

Band of Brothers (2001)
A ten-part story that follows a company of US paratroopers from D-Day to the Battle of the Bulge to the end of the war.

Websites

Search tips
Most sites are aimed at adults. They can contain upsetting information and pictures. Make sure that you use well-known sites with correct information, such as the ones below.

http://www.britannica.com/normandy
A look at Normandy in 1944.

http://www.bbc.co.uk/history/ww2children/index.shtml
Information about what life was like for children during World War II.

http://www.eyewitnesstohistory.com/w2frm.htm
This website is full of eyewitness accounts of World War II.

http://www.bbc.co.uk/dna/ww2
A good all-round site for the study of World War II.

http://www.awm.gov.au
The site of the Australian War Memorial.

Where to search

Search engine

A search engine looks through the entire web and lists all sites that match the words in the search box. It can give thousands of links, but the best matches are at the top of the list, on the first page.
Try **bbc.co.uk/search**

Search directory

A search directory is like a library of websites that have been sorted by a person instead of a computer. You can search by keyword or subject and browse through the different sites like you look through books on a library shelf. A good example is **yahooligans.com**

GLOSSARY

aircraft carrier huge ship with a flat deck that acts as a runway for naval planes to take off and land

alliance agreement to work together

Allies the group of nations that fought against Germany, Italy, and Japan

ammunition materials that are fired from a weapon

anti-aircraft guns weapons on the ground or on board ships that are used to fire at enemy planes

armistice formal agreement to stop fighting

artillery large guns that fire shells or missiles

battalion large military unit made up of 300 to 1000 troops

battle station a place for carrying out duties during an attack

battleship large and heavily armoured warship

bayonet long knife that is attached to the end of a gun

binoculars hand-held instrument that allows you to see distant objects

blockade using troops or warships to stop enemy soldiers or ships getting through to their destination

bunker a shelter from bombs that is usually underground

C-ration soldier's meal kit

camouflage material that is used to hide military equipment

campaign series of military missions

casualties people who are injured or killed in a war

civilian someone who is not part of the military

Communist someone who supports the political idea that government should own all land and industry

comrades friends

controversial open to dispute or debate

corporal soldier who ranks above a private but below a sergeant

crater huge hole left when a bomb hits the ground and explodes

democracy system in which people can elect their leaders

dictator person who has complete power over a country and is often cruel to those he or she rules

dive-bomber plane that flies at a target before releasing its explosives

divisions large military units consisting of about 10,000 men

evacuate bring to safety

foxhole shallow pit used for taking cover from enemy fire

grenades weapons filled with explosives that can be thrown at a target

howitzer cannon on wheels that is pulled into place by a tractor or jeep

infamy something that is famous for
being bad

Luftwaffe the German air force

monastery place where monks live
and pray

morale level of confidence and
determination to succeed

natural resources materials in nature
that are helpful to humans, such as
coal, oil, and minerals

Nazis people in the political party that
ran Germany from 1933 to 1945

Netherlands, the country in Western
Europe, also called Holland

paralysed physically unable to move

paratroopers soldiers who drop into
battle using parachutes

Parliament governing body of a country.
In the UK, it is made up of the House
of Commons and the House of Lords.

platoon a small army unit, usually made
up of 16 to 44 men

POW prisoner who is captured and put
in prison by the enemy during a war

resources useful materials, such as oil
or metals

sniper hidden soldier who shoots enemy
soldiers from long distances with a
special gun

Soviet Union country that once spread
across northern Asia into Eastern
Europe and included what is
now Russia. Also known as the USSR.

suicide act of killing oneself

supply routes paths used to transport
food, weapons, and other necessary
items

Supreme Court top legal institution in
the United States

torpedo missile that is fired underwater

trip-wire wire that is stretched close to
the ground and acts as an alarm if
someone touches it

U-boat type of German submarine

wingmen pilots who fly behind the
leader of a flying formation of planes

work camps places where people were
forced to live and work for little
or no money

INDEX